VIA Folios 63

Chianti in Connecticut

Other Books by Gil Fagiani

Crossing 116th Street, Skidrow Penthouse (2004)
Rooks, Rain Mountain Press (2007)
Grandpa's Wine, Poets Wear Prada (2008)
Vino del nonno, Italian translation of Grandpa's Wine by Paul D'Agostino,
Poets Wear Prada (2010)
A Blanquito in El Barrio, Rain Mountain Press (2009)
Serfs of Pyschiatry, Finishing Line Press (forthcoming 2011)

Acknowledgements

"Paradiso," *Italian-Americana*, Number 1, Winter 2009.

"American Now," "Figaro," "Mariuzza," *Grandpa's Wine*, Poets Wear Prada, Hoboken, New Jersey, 2008.

"Footware for Freaks," *Writing Outside the Lines*, edited by Tammy Nuzzo-Morgan, forthcoming 2010.

"A Sicilian in Potter's Field," *Paterson Literary Review*, No. 33, 2004 and *Feila-Festa*, Spring, 2007.

"The Saint," *Remembrances*, edited by Edward Maruggi, Hilton, NY, 2009.

"Chicky," *Gravida*, Number 34, Fall 2008.

"Freddy's Father," *Identity Theory*, Issue 36, 2006.

"Bad Boy Pete," "Why I became an Atheist," *Fox Chase Review*, Autumn/Winter 2009.

"Agates," *Shot Glass Journal*, Issue 1, 2010.

Earlier versions of "Chianti in Connecticut," appeared in *Paterson Literary Review*, Number 31, 2002, *Feila-Festa*, Spring 2006, and *Grandpa's Wine*, Poets Wear Prada, Hoboken, New Jersey, 2008.

Dedicate alle famiglie: Cangemi, Diserio, Fagiani e Fiocco

Ever get the
Feeling that your past
Is a hunter who knows the
Woods better than you

"Four Untitled"
New and Collected Poems, 1964-2007, Ishmael Reed

Table of Contents

The Cerelli Brothers

Shanz's Paint And Hardware

About the Author

Chianti in Connecticut

Paradiso

Ninna-nanna, ninna-nanna,
Nonna sings
bouncing her laughing
fat-cheeked
naked
grandson
on her knee.
She stops
grabs one of his ears.
I'll eat a piece of this!
The boy giggles.
Nonna begins bouncing again,
ninna-nanna, ninna-nanna.
She stops
grabs his nose.
I'll eat *un pezzu di chistu!*
The boy giggles
Nonna sings,
ninna-nanna, ninna-nanna.
She stops
grabs his chin.
Manciu un pezzu di chistu!
The boy reaches down
with both hands
grabs the little worm
between his legs.
Eat this, grandma!
Nonna slaps his hand,
laughs.
Oh, you fresh-a boy,
ninna-nanna, ninna-nanna.

Good-Bye Bronx

American Now

Looking down
from the elevated line
of the Sixth Avenue subway
Tina watches the dark streets
of Greenwich Village vanish
into Old World memories.

She is happy to go
happy to speed away
from mamma's
nervous eyes
and Sicilian war cries
away from alleyways
reeking
of fruit and fish
and guinea stinker cigars
away from pinching cousins
bristly moustaches
and barber shops
buzzing
with the Babel
of a dozen dago dialects.

Tina speaks American now
smells American now
looks American now.

The sole sign
of her immigrant home:
the pierced
gold heart earrings

her grandmother
sent her from Messina
she throws
out the subway window.

Figaro

Saverio, you were hard as the heels
you put on the shoes you made
all glue and nails and stiff strips of leather.
You ordered us around
never any question
never any doubts
like *un buon figlio*
you answered only to your mother.

When the eels ran off City Island
you bustled into the kitchen
with brown paper shopping bags
squirming with *anguille.*
You chased out the woman folk
snatched the eels by their tails
and hammered their heads on the floor
till their eyes turned to jellied diamonds.

Then you stuck their necks
onto a square masonry nail
high above the stove
pulled off their skin
and after a deep knife slash in the belly
ripped out a balloon bag of guts.

After quartering the eels
you beat eggs in a bowl with your fingers
dropped the pieces into the frothy mix
rolled them over some flour
and threw them into a frying pan
sizzling with olive oil.

7

Once I walked into the kitchen
and saw eel body parts
dancing in a black skillet
while you sang a refrain
from Mozart's "Figaro."

Fireflies

As soon as she arrives
in an Arctic fox collar
everyone knows—
after all, Aldo manages
the fur department at Macy's—
and it's no secret
he has a *comare,*
a woman on the side.

But no one would have thought,
least of all my father,
who like the rest of his relatives
wouldn't admit to a thing
when it came to the sins of his family,
nobody would have believed Uncle Aldo
with his impeccably-tailored suits
his salmon pink cheeks
his soft eyes
would have the *coglioni*—the balls—
to invite his mistress
to his daughter's wedding party.

But there under starlight
as his wife ferries food
from the kitchen to the patio,
Aldo waltzes, cha-chas
with his girlfriend
while my father's family
stares at fireflies.

Pouring a drink,
Aldo holds his glass high
and toasts the bride
who cleans the cigar ashes
off his tie before posing
with him for photos.

Later his *comare* says,
"The zitti was overcooked
and the cannoli half empty."
 "What do you want?" Aldo says,
"My wife's *calabrese*."

The Fruit Falls

When Saverio
sits at the table
he raps his wine glass
with his knife
when he wants something.
Ting ting!
and his wife Mariuzz'
leaps out of the kitchen
like a mad woman.
"Che cosa?" she asks.
Saverio looks at his mother
known as Za' Candida
who nods towards
the bread basket.
"Pane!" Saverio says.
And Mariuzz'
fetches the *pane*.
Ten minutes later.
"Ting ting!"
"Cosa?" Mariuzz' asks
her faced lined
like a butcher's block.
Za' Candida looks at
the empty wine pitcher.
"Vino!" Saverio says.
And Mariuzz'
fetches more *vino*.
At the end of the meal
Mariuzz' is at the sink
cleaning dishes
her niece Tina tangled

between her legs.
Za' Candida's eyes
roll heavenward.
Ting ting!
"Frutta!" Saverio yells.
Mariuzz' makes
the sign of the cross
grabs a bowl of fruit
trips over her niece
oranges in the air
like anarchist bombs.

November 6, 1945

Thousands throng the Grand Concourse
on crutches and wheelchairs,
others double park cars
drop to their knees in the street.

Their faces shine from the rain
falling like silt in the wobbly street light.
They arrange rosaries, flowers,
votive candles in the shape of a cross
under a stone cliff along 207th Street.

Every evening, a seven year-old boy
claims to talk to the Madonna,
who wears celestial blue
robes and a white crown.
It is said his touch has cured the blind,
removed cancerous rashes, healed
war wounds, helped polio victims
walk for the first time.

Suddenly he appears
pale-faced, eyes half-closed,
perched on the shoulders of his uncle
hair bouncing in ebony ringlets.

His face lights up
from hundreds of candles.
He lowers his head
and begins to pray.
Somebody yells that the rain
hasn't wet the boy's face.

Somebody else lets out a riff
of mocking laughter.

A gust of wind snuffs out the candles.
The crowd surges forward
grabs at his hands,
begging for a strand of his hair,
tearing the buttons off his coat.

The Romance of Helen Trent

Queen of the radio soap operas.
For twenty-seven years Helen has
proven, *what so many women long*
to prove in their own lives: that because
a woman is thirty-five, and more,
romance need not be over...

In all these years Helen has loved but one
man, the brilliant, incredibly handsome
lawyer, Gil Whitney, who chased her through
two decades of strife, refusing to give up
even when his war wounds
confined him to a wheelchair.

Thirty suitors chased Helen and when she
spurned them, they drugged her, beat her,
hypnotized her, pushed her off a cliff.
One jealous suitor shot Gil
when he sat in his wheelchair
and then tried to frame Helen.

In the last week, the production staff
killed off the main characters one by one:
Monday, a plane crash, Tuesday,
an amnesia seizure, Wednesday a landslide,
Thursday, a lightning bolt.

Finally, Friday, June 24, 1960
—my birth date, only 15 years later—
a balcony tumbles into a gorge
silencing Helen forever.

A knock at the front door.
A familiar voice.
"Helen! Helen"!—it's Gil."
Gil Whitney, the man my mother
named me after.

Good-Bye Bronx

with your hissing
steam pipes,
stick ball games,
fig trees in cement.
We're off
to the open spaces
of Springdale, Connecticut.

Behind the wheel
of the bullet-nosed
Studebaker Champion,
dad grins,
mom dabs tears,
I wave back at the mop
shaking out the tenement window.

In Reptilopia

Class War, 1955

A pointer swishes the air. "Get to work!"
I take out paper
draw a machine gun nest,
squadron of tanks, battery of howitzers.

Tommy's at the blackboard. "Wrong answer!"
The bombardment begins
shrapnel, rocks and sod fill the air
direct hits, dead soldiers everywhere.

My turn at the board. "Pay attention!"
Nails sink into my arms.
Returning to my seat, I sketch
jet fighters, missiles, billowing H bombs.

After class, my teacher gives me a note
for my mother to sign. "Doodles and
daydreams instead of working." I bury it
in the schoolyard with the rest of my artillery.

Footwear for Freaks

As a kid my folks made me wear
big boxy
orthopedic Oxfords
because the doctor told them
I had funny feet.

Other kids sported Keds, cordovans,
Buster Brown penny loafers,
saddle bucks, motorcycle boots,
while I walked around in
Bozo boats from hell.

Once I tripped over my Oxfords,
bashing my knee into a desk
after my fifth grade teacher shook me
in front of the class
for being a math moron.

The boys guffawed
the girls snickered
pain surged upwards
my face burned like
it had been drizzled
with sulfuric acid.

After school, I ran
to a nearby swamp
dammed up a creek
with rocks and clay
and built a water-bound playpen

where I chased salamanders and frogs,
pocketing a few before going home.

"I can't afford
to keep buying you shoes,"
my father laced into me,
my Oxfords drenched
and caked with crud.
He said he'd kill me
if I dared come home
with them muddy again.

Not long after, on a steamy
August afternoon
I took a bus to the beach.
A dash into the waves
a doze in the shade
then I dressed and strolled
to the old wooden latrines.

Two older kids jumped me
wrestled me to the ground.
"Now we have you, my little bambino,"
the taller one said,
pressing my nose like a doorbell.

Turning my pockets inside out
a speckled lizard scurried off.
The shorter boy leaped up
and tried to stomp it
then he pulled off one of my Oxfords,
"Freak!" he squealed
running into the latrine.

When I limped to that rotting toilet
and looked down the hole
stench socking the breath out of me
I could plainly see my Oxford floating

in a paper-rimmed lagoon
of shit and piss.

Back home, one foot shoeless,
my head hanging,
I slinked past my parents' stares,
opened my bureau draw
and stroked the toad
I'd hidden among my underwear.

Hanging Out with Older Bunch

At a small clearing
the youngest of the three
is sent to fetch brush
and soon a fire roars.

After warming a can
of Beeferoni, the older boys chow down,
saving a taste for the younger fellow
before breaking out a pack of Luckies.

As they cough and sputter
the older boys chat.
"You ever jack-off?"
"Nah, I'm scared, how 'bout you?"

"I hear you shoot blood!"
The younger boy smiles.
"What are you laughing at?"
the older boys shout.

They grab the youngster
by his arms and legs
swing him like a hammock
across the licking flames.

Then set him down
his dungarees fuming, tell him
to put out the fire, as they raise
their collars and walk away.

He's covering the coals
with frozen dirt, when he hears
voices fading, the distant
crackle of branches.

Mariuzza

Your husband called Mussolini
stronzaccio–big stinking turd–
in front of the *paesani*.

Your mother-in-law moved in
bullied your children
your brother moved out.

You sought relief working
in an East Harlem sweatshop.
Your mother-in-law collected your pay check.

Your son dropped out of school
committed insurance fraud
ended up in Sing Sing Correctional Facility.

Your daughter married
a half-wit sailor on VJ Day
and moved to Nebraska.

Your son-in-law hung himself.
Your daughter died of brain cancer.
You never saw your son again.

When your mother-in-law
and husband passed on
you lived on espresso and Brioschi

until you were a hundred and three.

Sign

Years before I knew
the brown bag Mrs. Gordon
carried up Weed Hill every day
came from the liquor store,
I remembered her son Tommy
in third grade
cutting a gingerbread man
out of cardboard
the week before Christmas
and stabbing it with a scissors
shouting, "Mommy! Mommy!
Mommy! Mommy!"

True Believer

President of the Bill Haley Fan Club,
you made me a disciple
and every Saturday morning
I tuned my dad's wooden Emerson
to "Make-Believe Ballroom,"
recording the Top Hundred Hits
in a loose-leaf notebook,
the room a riot of shrieking saxes
and rasping guitars.

We two-teamed rock's doubters,
scorned barbershop quartets,
opera sopranos, jazz buffs,
mambonicks, folk freaks.
Rock 'n' roll will never die
we boasted to our folks
who had to pry us from the family radio.

After being out of touch for years
I ran into you at a bus stop
and shouted my greeting
eager to show
my ever-lasting fidelity.
"The Bopchords!
Skip and Flip!
Reparata and the Delrons!"

You looked off into the distance,
bent your legs,
and clasped your hands together,
swinging upwards, "I'm into golf."

I was stunned.
You had expelled me
from the Bill Haley Fan Club
for "the girlie deviation,"
when I chased Candy Winns' pigtails
and Mimi Scott's pink-ribboned curls.

And while I leafed through my notebook,
memorizing the lyrics
to "Don't Knock the Rock,"
"Rock-A-Beatin' Boogie,"
you enlisted other followers.

Covers

Sister Mary Louis wears
a half-smile, and a cross on her belt
the size of a tomahawk.
Her eyes lock on to mine.
"Have you ever had impure thoughts?"

Everyone's head is down.
I shrink in my seat.
 "I'm talking to you.
Have you ever had impure thoughts?"
 "No," I blurt out.

"You've never looked at dirty pictures?"
"No."
"What about those French playing cards?"
"No, never!"

Out of the side of my eye
I see Candy's ripe lips
and Mimi's frilly collar.

"What about at night,
when you're in bed?"
My face burns.
My vision blurs.
Sister's smile broadens.

"Do you ever put your hand
under the covers?"
She knows! She knows!

Sweat frosts my armpits.
"No, no I don't!"

"You don't what?"
"Have impure thoughts."

In Reptilopia

I float on my back alongside
a flotilla of painted turtles

the shoreline aglow
with rainbow snakes and leopard frogs

In Reptilopia, tree frogs eat up
black flies and mosquitoes

peepers and bullfrogs play
cumbias, and concerti for double bass

alligators keep out bullies
and busybodies

The Dogs Were Racists

Friday Night Poker Game

Mom touches up her makeup,
puts out liquor bottles,
a can of peanuts, coasters,
glasses, fills the fridge with Rheingold,
shuts off the radio. Upstairs I hear
the doorbell, cheerful greetings.

Jimmy, ace woodworker, remodeled
our upstairs, smokes Di Nobilis, owns
the biggest house in the neighborhood,
his son quit high school, drives
a gold Studebaker Hawk
with leopard skin seat covers.

John, "Big John," washes down
scungilli with shots of Four Roses,
buys a new El Dorado every year,
people whisper he's a Mafioso,
bribing officials in the building
of the Connecticut Thruway.

Rocky, with the cool name,
like Rocky Marciano, makes flower
arrangements, always winking,
tells jokes that make my mother blush.
His wife's voice pierces the suburban
calm like a gang of blue jays.

Jake, salesman, the only non-
paesan in the crowd, with a soggy
smoker's voice, wags his finger,

warning me to behave. Once
he paid so his son and I could ride
the bumper cars all day at Rye Playland.

My father, shortest of the bunch,
chestnut eyes, model neatnik,
beats me with the buckle end of his belt
for messing up his work bench,
his hearty laughter makes me feel
I live with a stranger.

A Sicilian in Potter's Field

Uncle Dino lived incognito
in Corona for three decades.
The family says they don't know why.

A non-com in the Italian Army,
he followed Mussolini to Africa
for land and glory.
Maybe his spirit broke in Egypt
after five years in a British P.O.W. camp.

Maybe it was the bitter pill of work.
The only son, he was due
to run the family dry goods store
but his mother gave out too much credit
before the war ended
and the store went belly up.

Maybe it was a letdown in love.
His true blue was a *baronessa*
who was wild about him
but not so wild to buck her family
who made her marry
someone from her social class.

Maybe it was his brother-in-law
whom he lived with after he emigrated
from Sicily to New York
who bullied him like a child
and opened a letter from the *baronessa*
sending him fleeing from the Bronx.

But the family protests:
We tried to stay in touch.
He wouldn't give us his address
and when someone gave us
his telephone number
he wouldn't talk to us.

In the '70s, his sister Giovanna
even traveled from Sicily
and tracked him down
to a Corona rooming house
where he refused to see her
and told his landlord to send her away.

Among his *paesani*
one said, "could be he was a drug addict."
Another said, "could be he worked for the Mafia."
Still another, "could be he lived with a colored girl."

When Dino died in 1983
his landlord found a phone number
at the bottom of a seaman's bag
and called his niece Filomena
who called Giovanna.

"Maybe you should make arrangements
for his body to be brought back to Sicily."
Filomena said,
"Bada ai fatti tuoi!" Giovanna replied
—"Mind your own business!"
And Dino was taken away
in a City ambulance
and buried in potter's field.

Listening to "Peanuts" by Little Joe and the Thrillers

I see the emerald sheen
of a ring-necked pheasant

Gargle with sunshine

Do handsprings
in a field of apple blossoms

Chase cloud-shadows
along a path of pine needles

Backstroke in a sea
of beach ball marshmallows
bobbing in chocolate sauce

Christmas Vacation

I wanted to make up to Jerry
for what I did yesterday
when I stuck the muzzle
of my new air gun
into a mound of dog crap
and pulled the trigger
spattering shit
on his church-white shirt.

So I go with him to the candy store
with a pocketful of gift money
and on the way home
we stuff our mouths
with strawberry twists.
Jerry shakes his head
but I feed him more
until red drool streaks his face.

A pudgy kid pedals toward us
hunched over a girl's bicycle.
I see his big knuckles
and milky skin.
He's about to pass when I tell Jerry:
Spit in his face!
Jerry unloads a scarf of goo
on the kid's hair and face.

The kid drops his bike
and after a short chase
Jerry falls backwards to the ground
pawing the air

like an overturned beetle
as the kid's knuckles find his flesh,
blood, and licorice.

Saturday Afternoon

I go to the kiddie show
as rumors fly
our fathers are pressuring
the cops to close the State Theater,
claiming it's a hangout
for juvenile delinquents.

A third of the seats are filled
and after ten cartoons, the newsreel,
the Purple Monster serial, the Abbot
and Costello short, just as the second
Red Ryder flick is to begin, two boys
jump on stage with toy tommy guns.

Each fire off a roll of caps
the rat-tat-tat hammering
through the cavernous hall,
coils of smoke like nooses,
the boys vanishing in the shadows
slamming the exit door shut.

Fossils

We knew they existed
leaped out of our seats when teachers
used the word extinction.
Dinosaurs lived on, we insisted
deep in the Amazon jungle
and we swore nothing
would stand in our way
of tracking them down
not families, wives, or kids.

Being a Cub Scout, I argued,
and having a pet horned toad
made me a natural
expedition leader,
you said being a hall monitor,
President and founder
of the Bill Haley Fan Club
qualified you to be at the helm.

We argued if girls
should be allowed to join,
you said no, I wasn't sure,
should we pack guns?
I said no, you said yes,
should we bring a camera crew?
You said hell, yeah
—a Hollywood hit would
more than cover our expenses.

We fought over what we would do
once we ran into a pterodactyl

with its 40-foot wing span,
a stegosaurus, with its spiky-horned
tail, tyrannosaurus rex,
20 feet high, its six-inch teeth
serrated like steak knives.

You said drug them,
shackle their wings, limbs, tails,
ship them off to zoos,
I said let them roam free
behind giant barricades
in their home environment.

We argued until you transferred
to Catholic school and we didn't
see each other anymore,
leaving no trace
of our joint enterprise
except a cola-stained copy
of "Fifteen Questions Frequently
Asked about the Amazon Basin,"
and a plastic brontosaurus
missing a foot.

Vicious Virgins

As soon as we arrive
The peeping stops
Taking off our shoes
We wade into the pond
Feet tearing through plants
Long swaths of scum
Glisten on the surface
Below a tangle of arms and legs
Three, four, six male frogs
Clamped on to each female
We pick up the slimy clumps
Hurl them at each other
Water splashing, frogs flying
Arms speckled with tiny amphibian eggs

The Dogs Were Racists

The first time I saw a colored person
in Springdale in the 1950's
was when the new paperboy showed up.

The Hyatts affectionately
called him Sambo
kept their dog King,
a German Shepherd bitch
who wouldn't stop barking,
tied to the garage door.

They gave the boy Tootsie Pops
and Sugar Babies,
but he left in a week
without picking up
the money they owed him.

Then the colored garbage men came.
They jumped off a green truck
and were set upon by King
who broke his rope.

After being bitten in the ass
one of the men splashed
into the creek behind my yard
where Duke and Queenie snarled
from the other side.

The other man
swung a two by four
in wide circles

as King lunged
at the man's arms and legs
snapping his teeth.

When the police arrived
they weren't sure if they were called
to put down a rabid dog
or arrest two trespassers.

Grandpa's Notebook

To Carmelo Fiocco

It is not necessary to have exceptional ability.
Poise which gives power.
Poise which gives purpose.
Waste no time over vain regret.
"I lost my job, my savings, but
I sold fruit on street corners
to put food on my family's table."
Celebrate laughter.
Accept in the spirit of thankfulness.
Become accustomed to the necessity of action.
What a man feels makes him what he is.
"The Irish make fun of my accent
but they were shitting in the woods
when Romans sat on marble toilets."
Smile, smile, smile, never irritate.
Sloth is a daily purgatory.
Men prefer to traffic with people of more cheerful mien.
No one can exercise willpower for us.
"I made my own violin, guitar,
mandolin, studied Mozart, Beethoven,
played at Carnegie Recital Hall."
Work has the mark of divine appropriation.
Gentleness has the mark of the nobility of the soul.

The Cerelli Brothers

White-faced Mud Wasps

They lived alone in the dirt
by the brook behind Jerry's.
Their stings had already sent
two friends to the hospital
with arms swollen like inner tubes.

A veteran of insect bites,
I'd been stung by horseflies, bumblebees,
hornets. Once after stepping on their nest,
I was stung so many times by yellow jackets
Freddy scraped them off
with a piece of cardboard
stingers remaining like carpet tacks.

I'd survived squadrons
of flying demons, so I wasn't going
to get worked up by a few solo acts.

I was ten feet behind Jerry's house
—Connie next door
 was checking me out—
when two furry, lank bodies
landed inside my shirt collar.
At first they tickled like caterpillars,
but when I brushed them off they struck,
sending waves of fire across my body.

No honeybee, who dies after one sting,
the wasps jolted me and jolted me,
until hoarse from screaming,

I tore off my shirt and the wasps
detached from my flesh and flew away.

At least Connie never saw me
strapped to a gurney
and carted off to the emergency room
though the welts throbbed
like a barbwire collar
even under a heavy coat
of Calamine lotion.

The Saint

On Mott Street
she fed her future husband
chicken soup when he was feverish
and ignored by his family.

After they married
she didn't complain
about his tailoring apprenticeship
in York, Pennsylvania.

When he started working
she borrowed money
so they could buy a house
on Rochambeau Avenue in the Bronx.

Her brother-in-law
nicknamed her the saint
when she took him in and paid
his cab fare from Ellis Island.

In the halcyon days
of her husband's career
she would rise all hours of the night
to feed his cronies.

Rumors spread
that her husband's trips
to Newport, Rhode Island
were romantic trysts.

She gave birth to three sons
two died of spinal meningitis

before they could walk
and she doted on the survivor.

The day the Army ordered
him to leave for California
she fell out his bedroom window
to the sidewalk two floors below.

Her daughters said
it was an accident
but she spent six weeks
on a psychiatric ward.

After her discharge
she rarely spoke to her husband
spending her time silently
in their sun parlor.

At family dinners
she stayed in the back of the kitchen
while her daughters
served the guests their food.

I remember her waxen face
her shriveled shoulders
the dry lips that beaked my cheeks
and never formed a smile.

How hard she pulled
on her drunken husband's arm
at their 50th wedding anniversary
imploring him to sit
while he stood extolling her.

Scouting

I'm under a pup tent, giggling with a friend
the autumn air as snappy as the cider I swigged,
stars pulsing in the sky, "Be Prepared" the watch word,
tripping out on the Reptile and Amphibian merit badge
I earned, the swimming test I failed,
the fight I won by ramming my opponent's head
into the lean-to wall, mystery meat at dinner,
sleeping bag rumors of Scout Master molesters,
singing along to the Edsel's "Rama Lama Ding Dong,"
being ranked out by an Eagle scout, "the best
part of you ran down your father's leg."

Chicky

I spoke up for you
when the assistant principal
sent you home
for sporting a neckline
that sank too low,
took your side
when the history teacher
leered at you
lamenting chastity belts
were out of fashion,
stood up to my red-faced dad
when he called you a tramp.

Rumors had you luring boys
behind the stone incinerator
in the school yard
to jiggle their worms,
or down to the banks
of the Rippowam River
where you took off your clothes
begging to be mounted
on a bed of moss.

The nearest I came to you
was on Halloween Eve
when I stopped by your house
dressed like Zorro
and you lifted my mask,
"Let's peek
at the cute boy underneath."

At the church skating rink
my friend Phillip
tried to steal a feel,
by bumping into you,
and you snarled,
"Suck my dirty tits!"
your words
sending my hands churning
under the sheets
in a sticky lullaby.

I thought about you every night:
drowning
in the Long Island Sound,
I swam out and saved you,
dragged you
out of the back seats
of smoke-filled '50 Fords,
rescued you from the rear row
of the State Theater
where black-jacketed punks
took turns pawing you,
your gratitude
forever expressed
along the banks
of the Rippowam River.

Freddy's Father

had an anchor tattoo on his arm
and worked at the nearby rolling mill.
He didn't say much
but his wife made up for it,
usually at his expense.

"You have no manners,"
she'd say. "Close your mouth
when you eat, use your fork, not your fingers."
I had supper with them sometimes
and winced when Freddy
—their only child—would pile on.
"Slow down, dad, you eat like a horse."

One summer day, Freddy and I
were cooling off in his backyard,
hopping around the sprinkler,
while his father let us take turns
spraying each other with the garden hose.
I still had the nozzle in my hand
when he asked for it back.

Staring at his tattoo, I blasted
his shirt, his pants, his face.
"Hey, what the hell are you doing?" he said.
My fear gone, the thrill
of taking down an adult,
soaking him, until he grabbed me,
both of us slipping, wrestling
on our knees, on the ground.

Summer of '59

Mom called your clan *"cafoni"*
—ignorant louts—
your father a ditchdigger,
an ape, who could lift
a hundred-pound barbell with one hand,
wore a toupee, read comic books.

He never took his eyes off us
as we sat on the stonewall
separating Prudence Drive
from the woods beyond.

My guts buckled like tar
in the August heat as I saw
your sprouting nipples, rounding hips
tan that lingered when the summer left.

We talked for hours
your voice dusky
like your hair, eyes, skin
the mystery of your darkness
keeping me awake at night.

In the evening I would call you
the telephone lines crackling
as we made plans to meet in the woods
where a spread of clover
made for a natural mattress.

You sighed while I described
how I'd undress you

61

doing to you what the boys
did to Chicky,
the neighborhood nymphomaniac.
The next day I'd be there
but you never showed up.
Your folks never let you out of their sight
you claimed, your eyes glowing.

When the summer ended
you invited me to a dance.
I didn't know any steps,
feared I'd lose control
with your body next to mine.
Instead I jogged for miles
dreamed of making the football team.

A month before we stopped speaking
my father said he'd break my neck
if I ever brought you into the woods,
his words spat out like sizzling bacon fat.

The Cerelli Brothers

We wake to ripsaws and hammer blows.
Joe Cerelli says working in the sun makes him black as a jigaboo.
Toads and box turtles die under the bulldozer's treads.

We spider web their truck windows with mortar chunks.
Big John Cerelli stuffs the mailman's face in his sack for staring at his wife.
We steal planks, nails, tarpaper and build a tree fort.

Frank Cerelli's son is left back in the 9th grade for the second time.
I fake a limp when Big John's daughter invites me to the C.Y.O. dance.
The Cerelli Brothers rout the brooks into pipes and culverts.

The wild turkeys disappear along with trout and pussy willows.
Joe Cerelli's dog Prince drowns in his Roman swimming pool.

The Butterfly Bush

In spring
a lilac bush
blossomed alongside
the Kawalski's brick house
at the end of Prudence Drive.

Flowers
big and purple
scented the air
with a heady sweetness
attracting butterflies
in the neighborhood.

Monarchs,
tiger swallowtails,
regal fullinaries,
tawny emperors,
and painted ladies,
landed on one bush.

Jerry, Freddy, and I
would trap them in nets,
asphyxiate them in fruit jars
with cleaning fluid
then flatten their wings
in a dictionary
and mount them
in small wooden frames.

The three of us
attacked that bush

from sunset to sundown
first as a group
but later, when the canker
of greed got the best of us,
we mostly made
solo raids.

From the start the Kawalskis
whose daughter Marisha
we teased for being
ugly and flat-chested
cursed us
complaining about damage
to their lawn, flowers, and shrubs.

We fought back
blizzarding their yard
with newspaper scraps,
hanging on telephone poles
profiles of Marisha
with titties
like concave cupcakes,
setting brown bags on fire
on their front stoop
filled with dog doo
so that when Mr. Kawalski
stamped them out
he'd get shit on his shoes.

It went on
even when we grew
bored with butterflies,
it went on
until Mrs. Kawalski had a stroke,
her twisted face,
garbled talk,
her dragging
dead leg,
frightening us away.

Haunted Houses

Freddy coasts in a cherry-red Raleigh
with gears and handbrakes.
Jerry and I pump Schwinns
with truck fenders and balloon tires.

He leads us to deserted houses.
One nearby is gutted.
He salvages garden tools
while we break the spindles
on the staircase railing
pull down the living room ceiling.

He finds a Victorian house
behind a cornfield
that takes an hour to reach.
He gathers picture frames,
brass doorknobs, leather-bound books.
We break windows, dishes,
splinter chairs and tables.

Silently he rolls up rugs,
collects vases, mirrors,
silverware, kitchen utensils.
We chant "Papa-Oom-Mow-Mow"
and tear off cabinet doors,
rip down curtains,
pull out faucet plumbing.

He stashes his findings in the cellar.
The three of us make extra trips
to bring everything home,

Jerry and I always take the occasion
to stomp bureau drawers,
smash tile and porcelain.

By the time the police board up the house
our hands are covered
with cuts and splinters
while Freddy has the start-up stock
for his future antique store.

Shanza's Paint and Hardware

Motherless

I knew—everyone knew—
Timmy was being raised
by his dad, a night watchman
in a meatpacking plant.

Buried in the slowest classes,
I didn't see much of him
except one year in Junior High
when we were in the same homeroom.

I recall the spaces where teeth
should have been, the shaggy hair,
how he held his breath
to make his chest look bigger.

Before the teacher took roll
he used to rant about America
being too soft with the Russkis
and how we shouldn't buy
anything foreign-made.

Once at a track meet,
some rival fans ripped up
our school banner.
Timmy charged the culprits
—Negroes from Portchester.

One knew how to box, bloodied
Timmy's nose, closed one of his eyes.
Still Timmy wrestled him to the ground,
sat on his back, grabbed his springy hair,

and smashed his face into the cinder track
until a referee tore him off.

When he dropped out of sight
I had him working in a circus
running the Tornado,
or in the Special Forces
slitting throats behind enemy lines,
or a salad man in a fleabag hotel
in the Catskills.

Listening to "Deserie" by the Charts

I hear the tiger's steps
before it pounces

see the soaring osprey
a steelhead in its claws

taste the spring grass
on the scythe's blade

I feel the stalactite's
icy drip

the flutter
of a thousand bat wings

the tumble of the tide
onto the silver seaweed

Shanz's Paint and Hardware

In first grade Lenny broke a girl's jaw
for calling him a retard.
His father locked him up in his room
and never let him go to school again.

Years later, Carl Shanz hired Lenny,
a muscular six-footer, to work
in his warehouse where he shoveled sand
into paper bags for mixing cement
and loaded and unloaded bricks,
cinderblocks and fertilizer.

Afraid to use a step-ladder,
Lenny once jumped up to grab
a gallon can of paint from a shelf
when it tumbled down, leaving
a dent-scar in his forehead.

The summer before
I started military college,
Shanz hired me as a clerk
to help Lenny in the warehouse.
Before leaving, I got my jollies
by torturing Lenny.

I'd telephone him
and laugh like Boris Karloff
in *"The Mad Ghoul,"*
or use a rubber band slingshot
to fire iron staples
at the aluminum roof of the warehouse

that made a bang like a gun shot.
Lenny would bolt outside, hair wild,
eyes like a horse's in a barn fire.

The week before I donned cadet grays
I poured lighter fluid around
a sand pile Lenny was working on
and threw a match when his back was turned
trapping him in a circle of fire.

After the flames burned down
and Lenny's howls stopped
Mr. Shanz chewed him out
for soiling himself
and sent him home without pay.

That afternoon, I took Lenny's place
in the warehouse
where I pulled a ligament
lowering a 90-pound cement bag
in a car trunk. At school
I marched on the parade grounds
trussed in a back brace.

Bad Boy Pete

In eighth grade
when asked, "How's Bella?"
Pete sniffed
his middle finger
and said, "Fine!"

In ninth grade
he asked Mrs. Hickey
in our bio class
about her second set of lips.
In Porky Mason's
print shop class
he hid his marking book
stole a font of ink
smearing it on our bus driver's seat.

In tenth grade
he hung out in the front row
of the auditorium
with the colored girls
and lip-synched
"Daddy's Home"
by Shep and the Limelites
later bragging
'bout getting
plenty poontang.

In eleventh grade
Pete cheated on every exam
tampered with the line of scrimmage
at football games

shot out school windows
with slingshots and marbles
flushed cherry bombs
down toilets
engulfing hallways in feces
his lawyer father
having him reinstated
every time he was suspended.

In twelfth grade
he piped the Olympics'
"Bad Boy Pete"
into the school's loud speaker system
paid Brain-Job Brancatelli
to take his SATs
switched his graduation partner
so he picked up his parchment
with the Senior Prom Queen.

Pete attended Columbia
peddled triple X gelatin capsules
of horse tranquilizer
cigarettes dipped in embalming fluid
flunked out
and shortly afterwards
was found
in the front closet
of the 80 year-old paraplegic
aunt he was staying with
in New York City
with his head
cut off.

Agates

After the war
my father came home
with rocks cut in half
outsides drab and craggy
insides polished to glass.
Staring at cloudy shapes
behind window-like surfaces,
I think about my father:
A blue tyrannosaurus
with a frog on its shoulder,
a baying dog with his back
covered in flames.

Why I Became an Atheist

At fifteen
I got on my knees every night
praying Connie
would come back to me.

I prayed to God Almighty
unseal my lips
give me the power
to persuade her to return.

I prayed to the Holy Ghost
bestow upon me
the grace that would make
her mine again.

I prayed to the Virgin Mary
with her beseeching look
to fill my ex-girl
with yearning for me.

I prayed to Jesus Christ
to raise our romance from the dead
promising I'd quit whipping
my wood in Connie's name.

After two weeks nothing—
no convincing words
no longing in my ex's heart
no heavenly resurrections.

Chianti in Connecticut

Grandpa liked the sun
and sat in our backyard
in an aluminum beach chair
reading *Il Progresso Italo-Americano*
smoking cigars
with his name on the wrapper
and drinking his wine.

He drank it
from fancy glasses
punch glasses
empty peanut butter jars
fruit jam jars
poured it
over berries
peach slices
crumbled cookies
tapioca pudding.

It was Freddy who told me
Italians only built brick houses
blew their nose through their fingers
and had tempers.
He said he saw an Italian laborer
—part of a work gang
laying water mains on Hope Street—
shit in a ditch
in front of oncoming traffic.

My grandfather was once
un pezzo grosso—a big man

in the Italian community—
designing fur coats for models
and Hollywood stars
his banquets attended by *prominenti*
covered in all the Italian newspapers
in New York.

His family adored him,
not a word of criticism
would they tolerate,
even though his wife jumped
out the window—my mother said—
to end her servitude
to his high-handed ways.

Sometimes I would look at him
sitting for hours in a beach chair
despised by his daughter-in-law
polluting the Connecticut countryside
with the reek of Chianti
and his fat Italian cigars.

Back in the Bronx

staring at the side
of my old tenement
with the faded outline
of a tobacco ad:
a dolphin-skulled giant
wearing a top-hat
puffing a pipe
the bowl like a swollen testicle
the smoke like a swarm of bees.

Jackasses

Castelbuona, Sicily

Sign on the castle door
reads "*Chiuso* – Closed!"
I return to my car
parked on the mountain's edge.
Three donkeys graze,
tails swatting waves of flies
on their ears, lips, genitals.
One donkey—perhaps in heat—
keeps ramming his head
into the rear of another.

Italian class, Mr. Franchina
face flushed, yelling:
"*Asini! asini!*—jackasses!"
We were
—but we were good-looking asses.
Dark eyes, mops of curly hair,
bulging muscles, and girls
with breasts, hips—*mamma mia*—
who could focus on indirect objects,
when legs crossed, flesh trembled.

Aroma, the sounds
of tearing underbrush.
The donkeys find wild fennel,
chew on the tender top shoots
their teeth grinding side to side.

About the Author

Gil Fagiani's poetry collection *Rooks* is set at Pennsylvania Military College in the 1960s (Rain Mountain Press, 2007); his chapbook, *Grandpa's Wine* (Poets Wear Prada, 2008), which focuses on his family's immigrant generation, has been translated into Italian by Paul D'Agostino. The backdrop for *A Blanquito in El Barrio* (Rain Mountain Press, 2009) is the streets and music of Spanish Harlem. His chapbook *Serfs of Psychiatry* is due to be published by Finishing Line Press in 2011.

Fagiani has read his poetry on WNYC during National Poetry Month and has translated into English, poetry written in Italian, Abruzzese dialect, and Spanish. His poems and translations have been published in more than a dozen anthologies, and have appeared in *The New York Times*, *The Paterson Literary Review*, *Mudfish*, *Skidrow Penthouse*, *Descant*, *Philadelphia Poets*, *Identity Theory*, *Saint Elizabeth Street*, and *The Ledge*.

He co-hosts the monthly open reading of the Italian American Writers Association at the Cornelia Street Café, and is the Associate Editor of *Feile-Festa: A Literary Arts Journal*. Fagiani is a social worker (L.C.S.W.) and addiction specialist (C.A.S.A.C.) by profession, and has directed a residential support program for recovering alcoholics and drug addicts in Downtown Brooklyn for the last 20 years.

VIA FOLIOS

A refereed book series dedicated to Italian studies and the culture of Italian Americans in North America.

Published by BORDIGHERA, INC., an independently owned not-for-profit scholarly organization that has no legal affiliation to the University of Central Florida or the John D. Calandra Italian American Institute, Queens College, City University of New York.

JONE GAILLARD CORSI
Il libretto d'autore, 1860–1930
Vol. 12, Criticism, $17.00

HELEN BAROLINI
Chiaroscuro: Essays of Identity
Vol. 11, Essays, $15.00

T. PICARAZZI & W. FEINSTEIN, EDS.
An African Harlequin in Milan
Vol. 10, Theater/Essays, $15.00

JOSEPH RICAPITO
Florentine Streets and Other Poems
Vol. 9, Poetry, $9.00

FRED MISURELLA
Short Time
Vol. 8, Novella, $7.00

NED CONDINI
Quartettsatz
Vol. 7, Poetry, $7.00

A. J. TAMBURRI, ED. & M. J. BONA, INTROD.
Fuori: Essays by Italian/American Lesbians and Gays
Vol. 6, Essays, $10.00

ANTONIO GRAMSCI
P. VERDICCHIO, TRANS. & INTROD.
The Southern Question
Vol. 5, Social Criticism, $5.00

DANIELA GIOSEFFI
Word Wounds and Water Flowers
Vol. 4, Poetry, $8.00

WILEY FEINSTEIN
Humility's Deceit: Calvino Reading Ariosto Reading Calvino
Vol. 3, Criticism, $10.00

PAOLO A. GIORDANO, ED.
Joseph Tusiani: Poet, Translator, Humanist
Vol. 2, Criticism, $25.00

ROBERT VISCUSI
Oration Upon the Most Recent Death of Christopher Columbus
Vol. 1, Poetry, $3.00